world of beauty

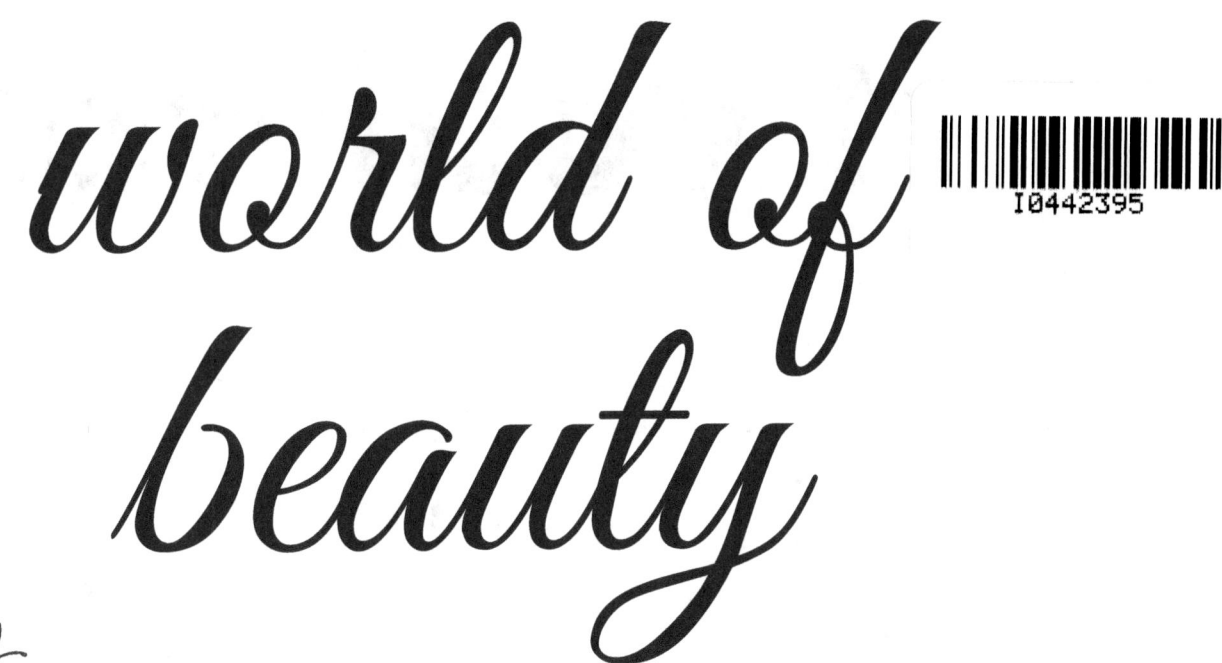

this coloring book belongs too

. . . .

test your color

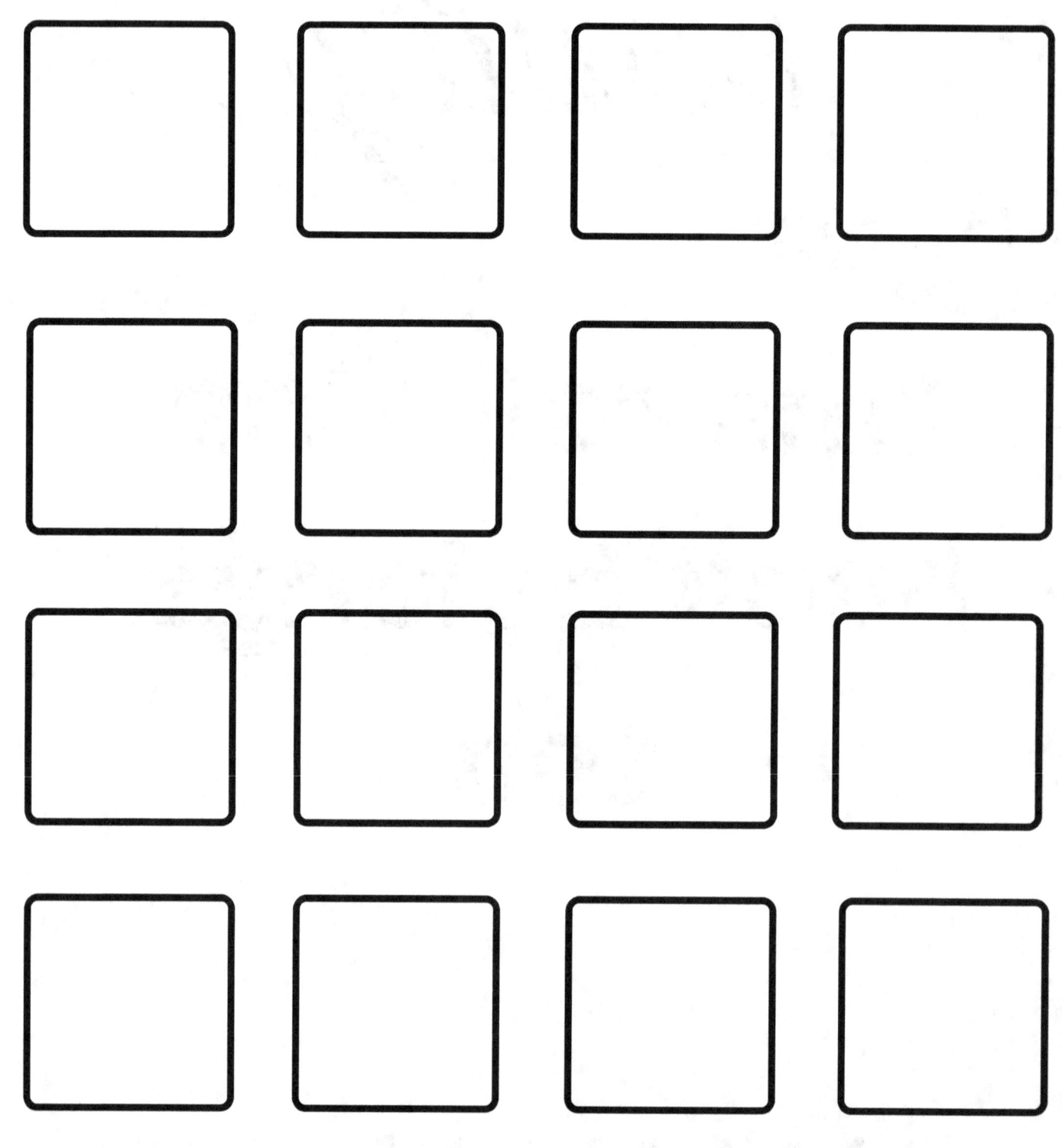

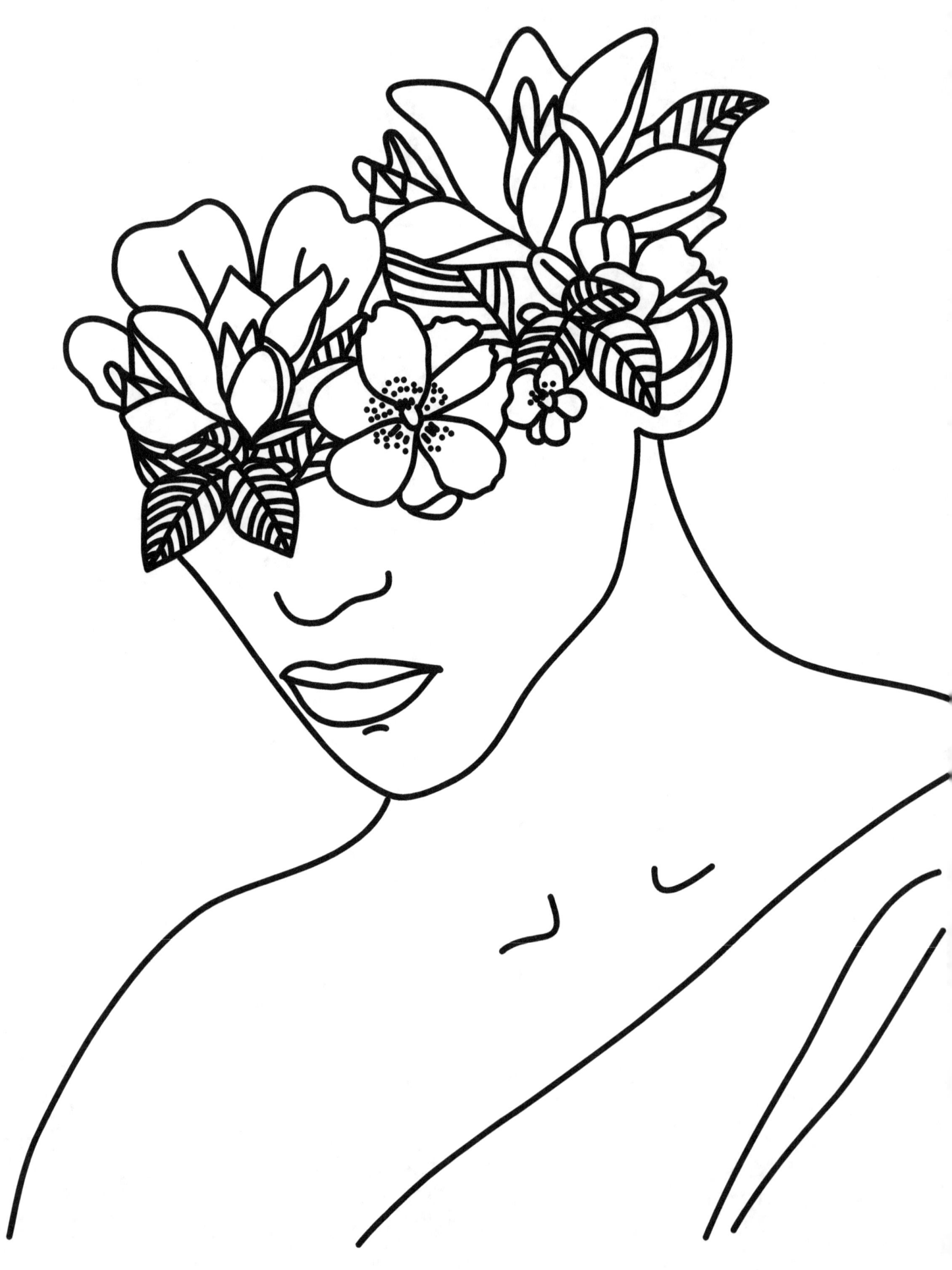

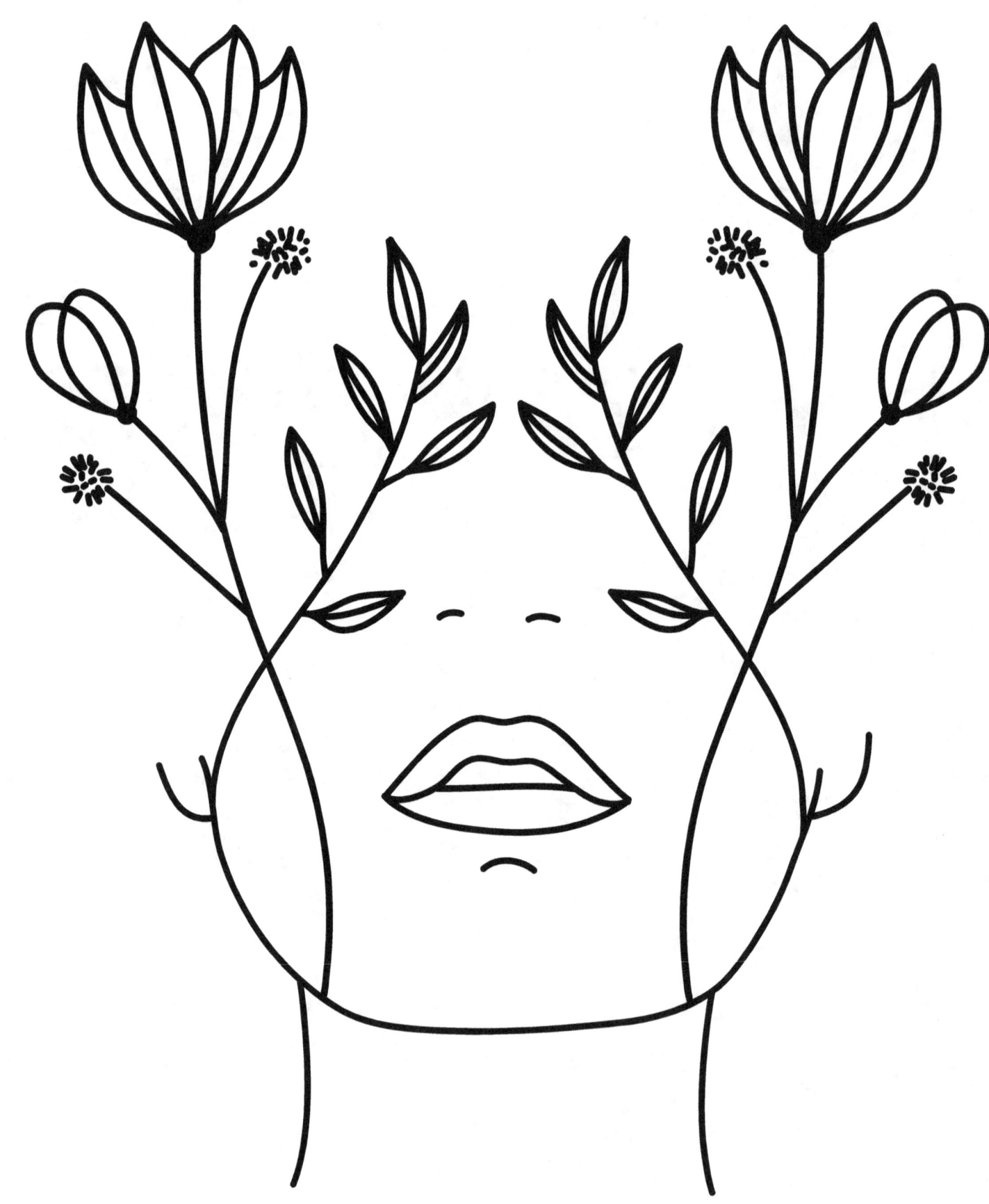

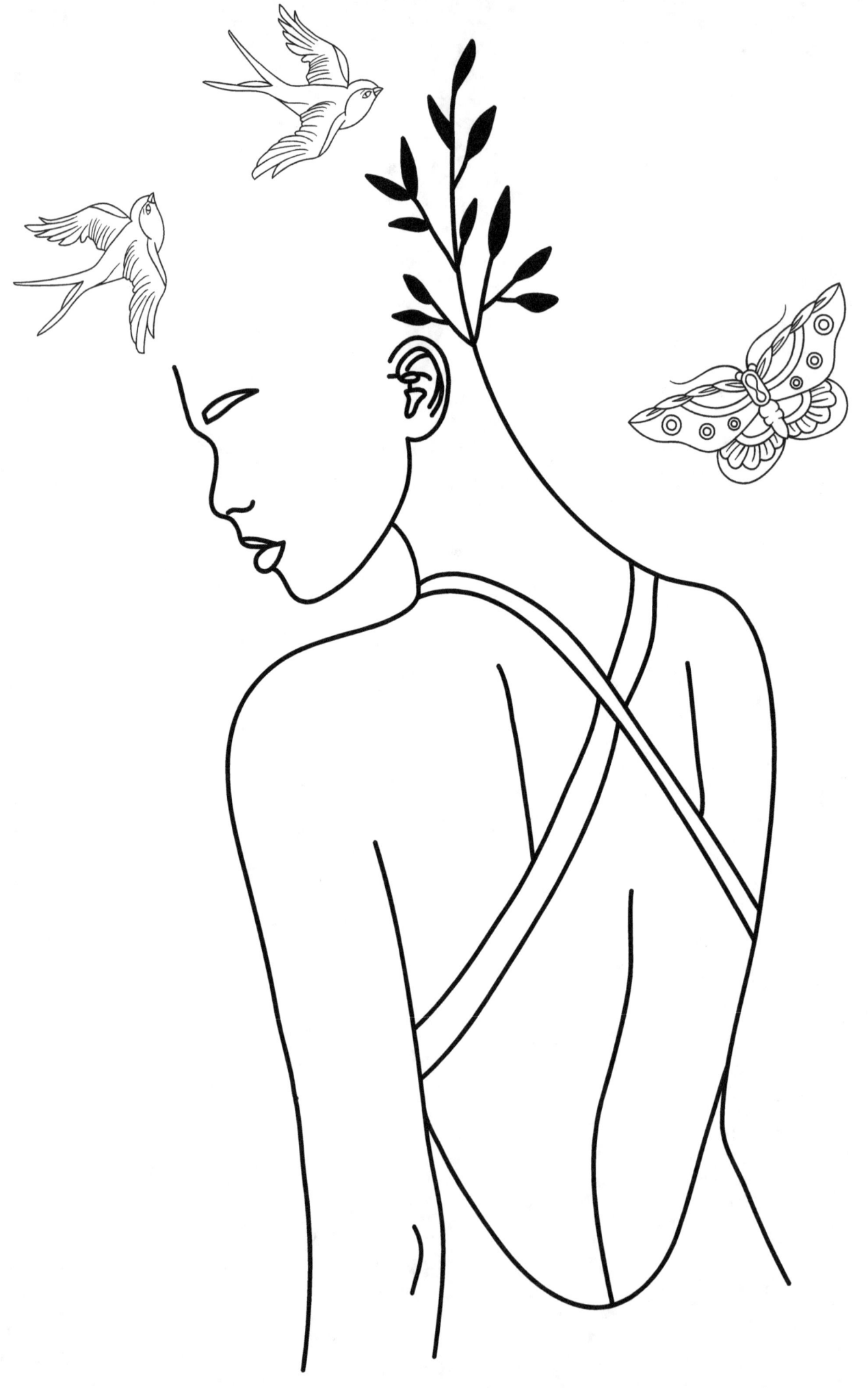

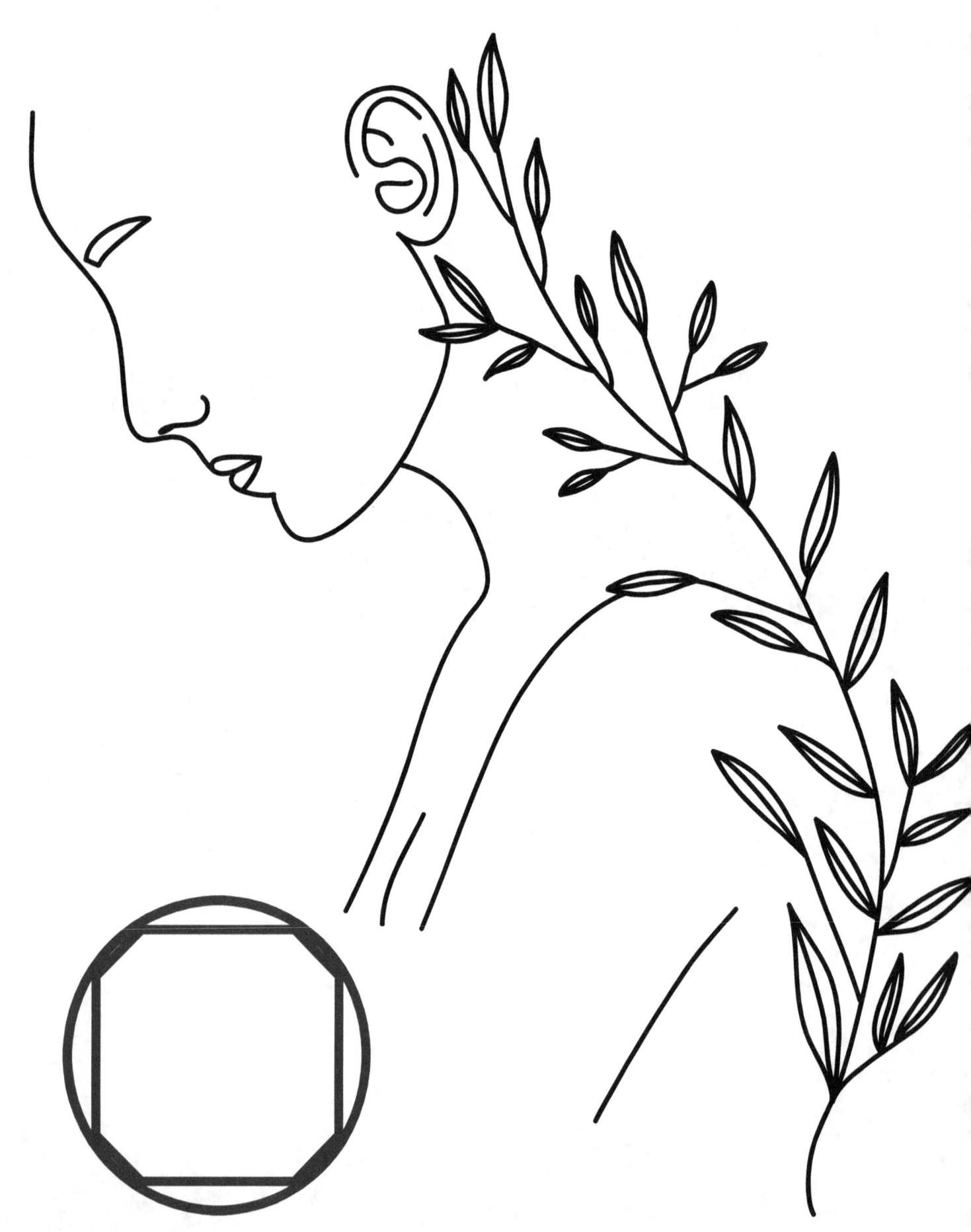

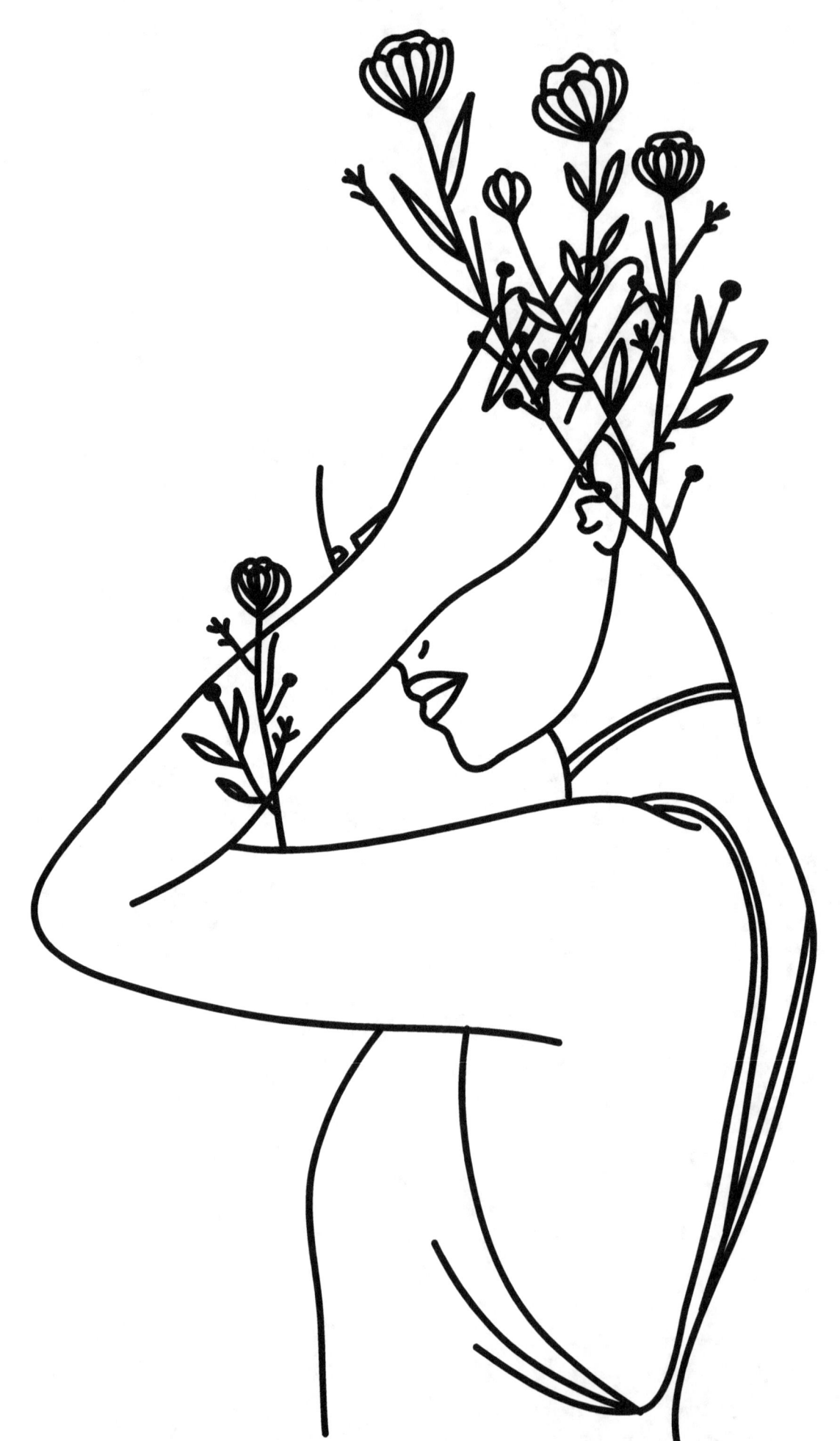

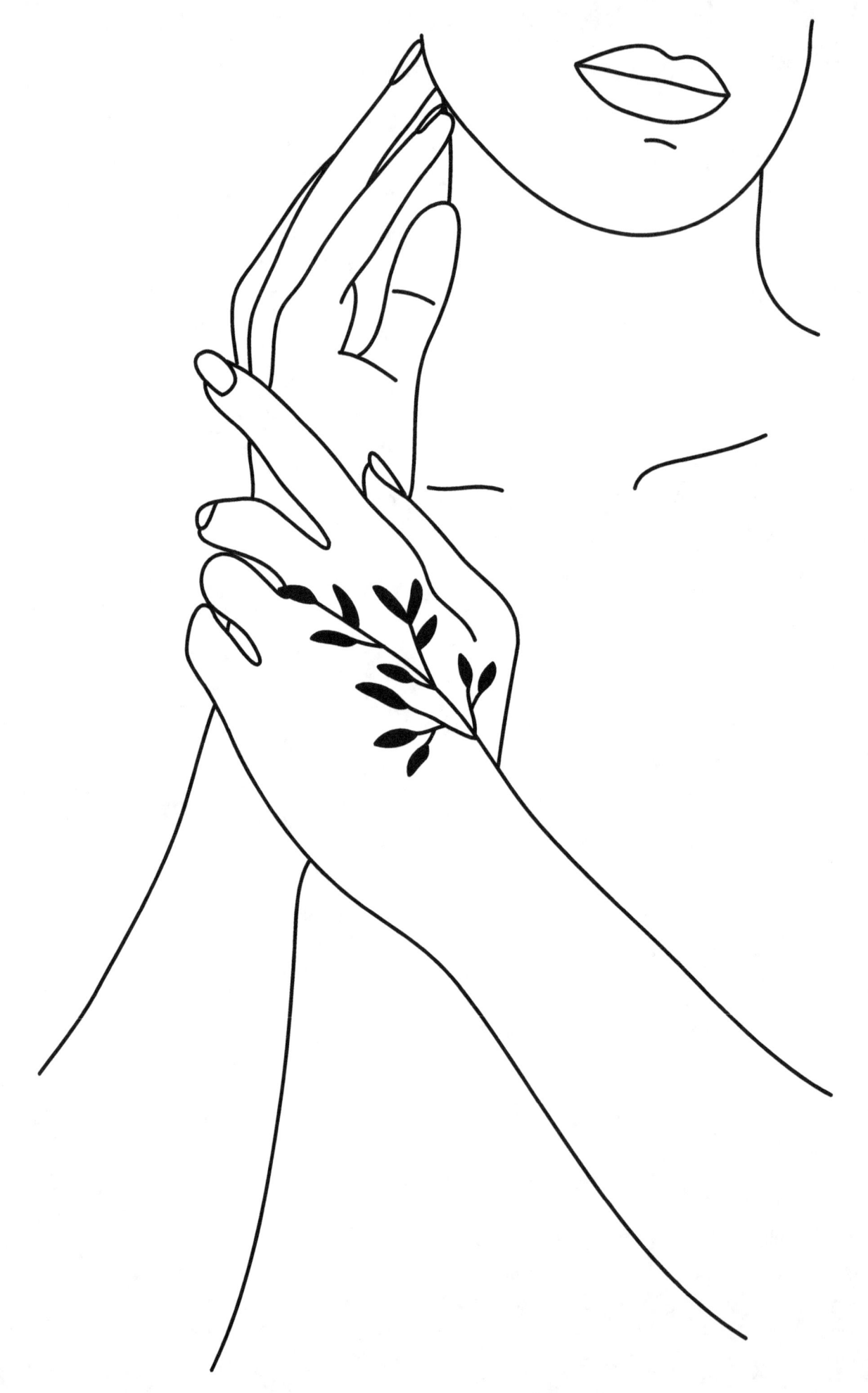

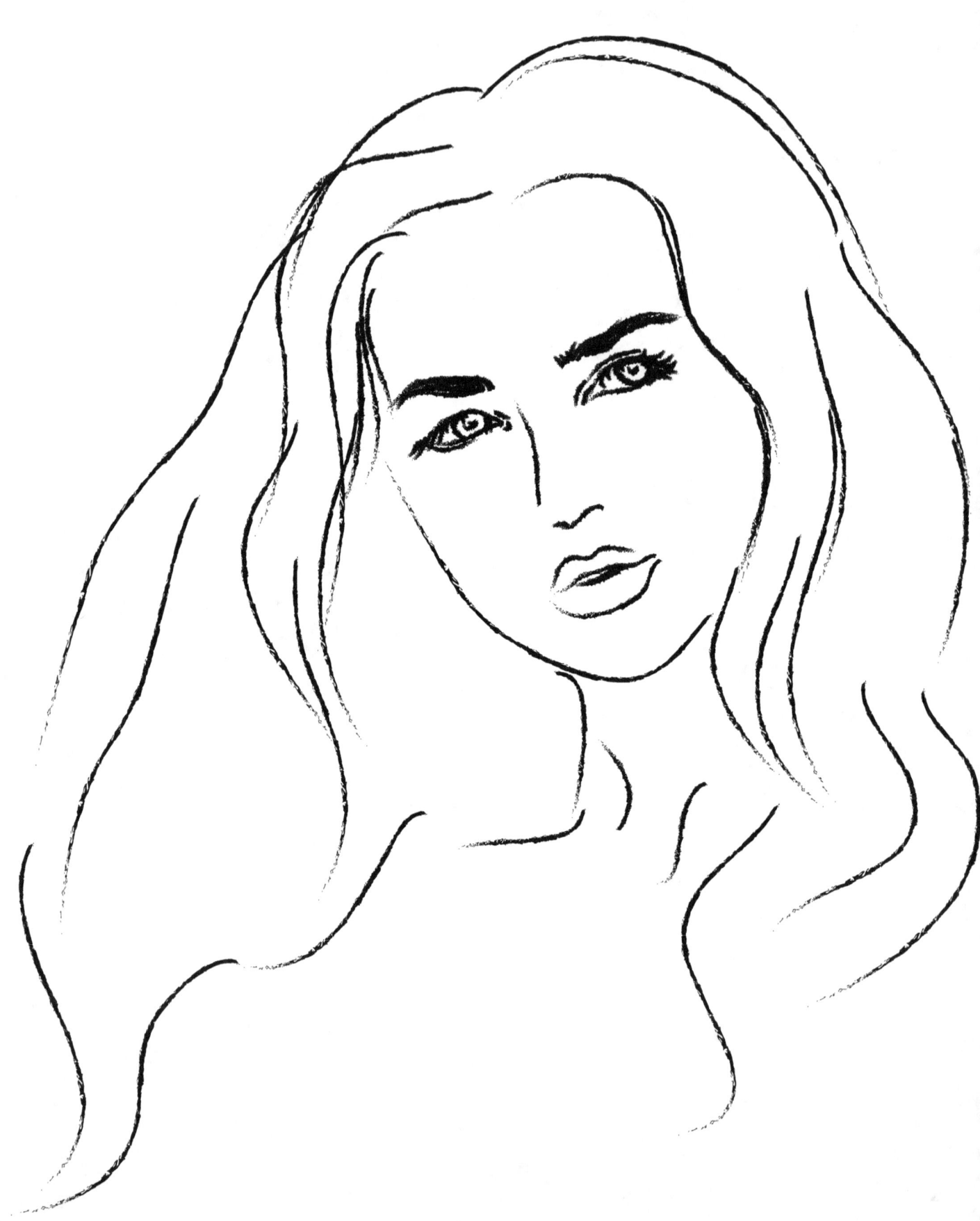

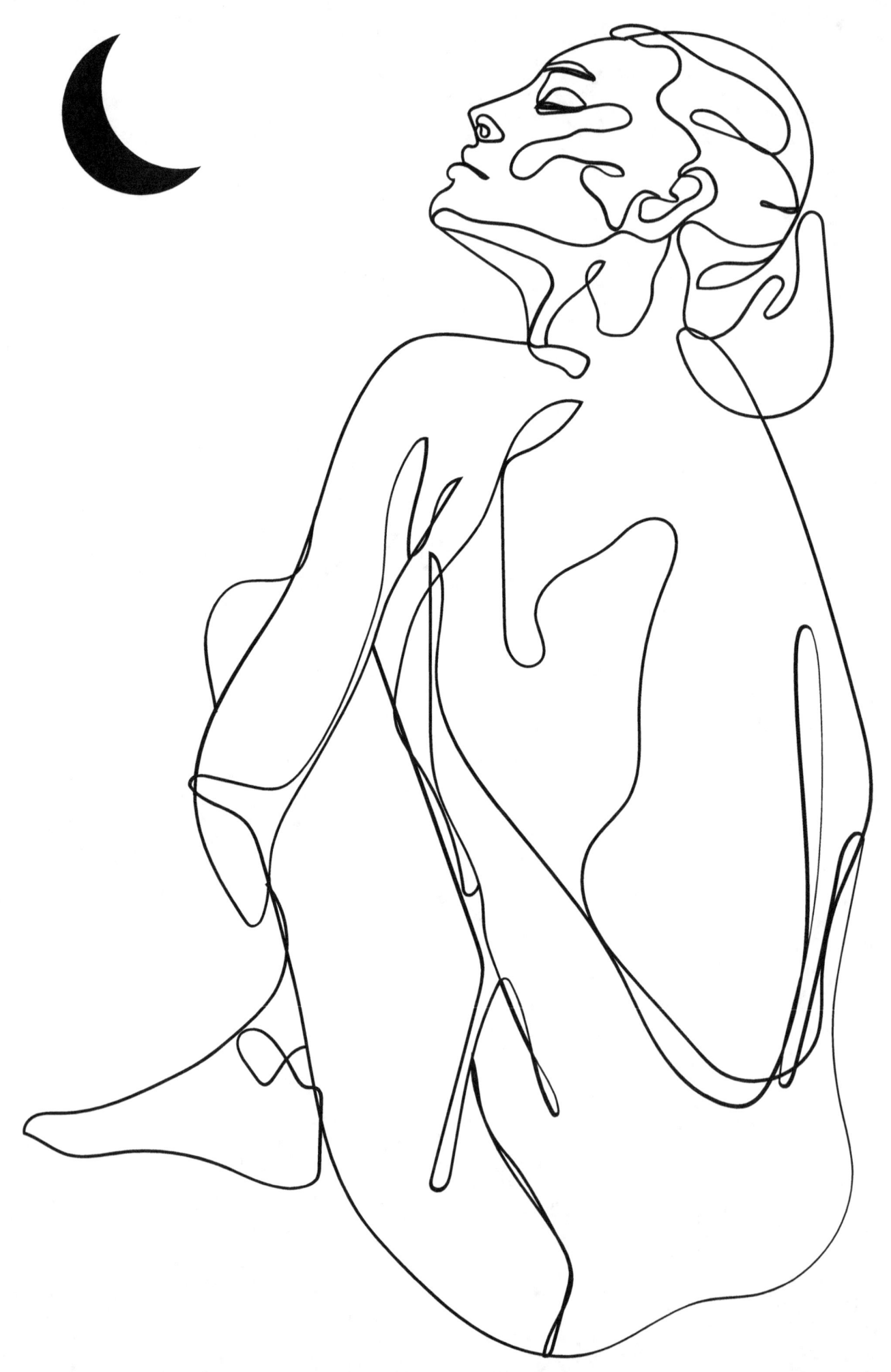

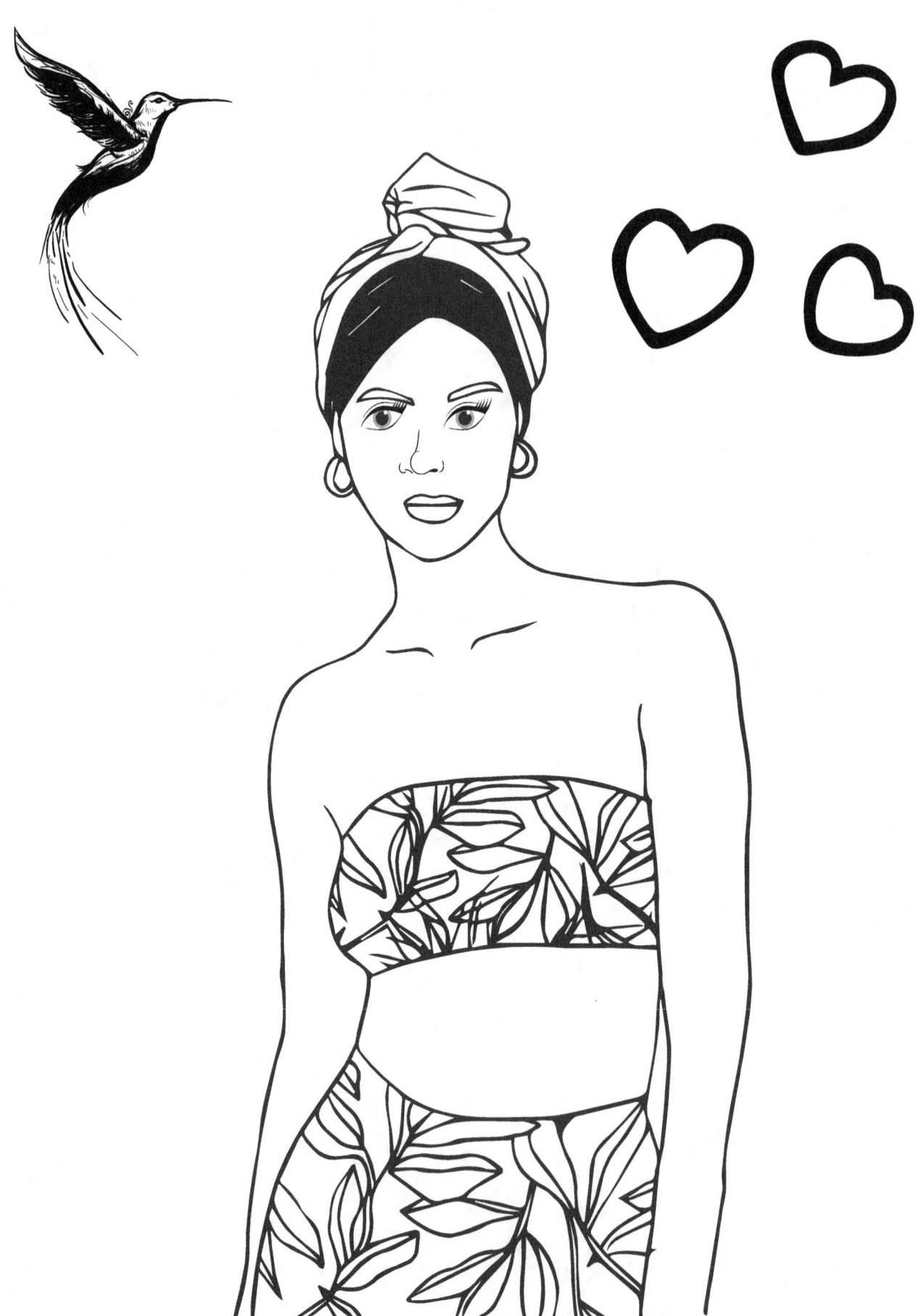

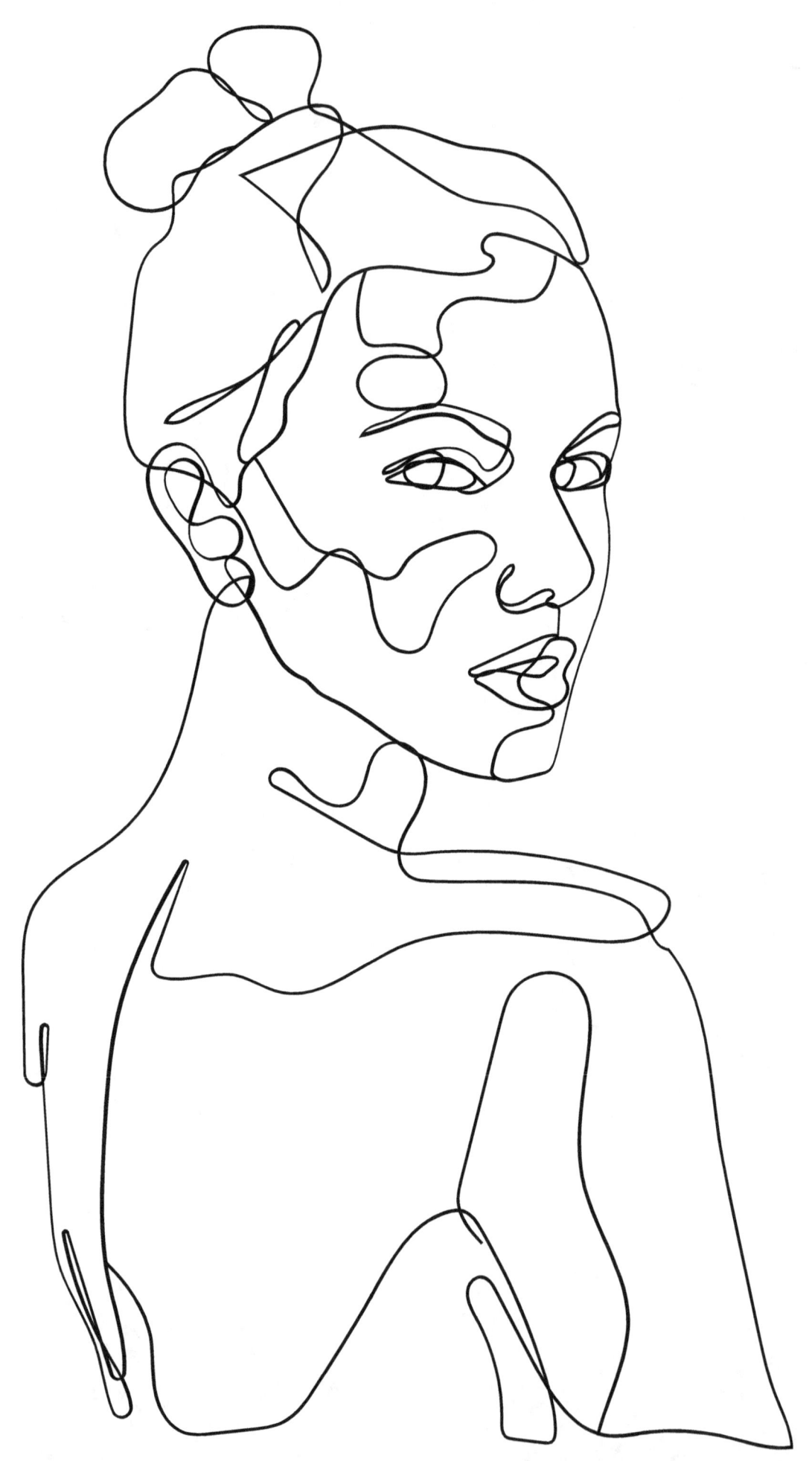

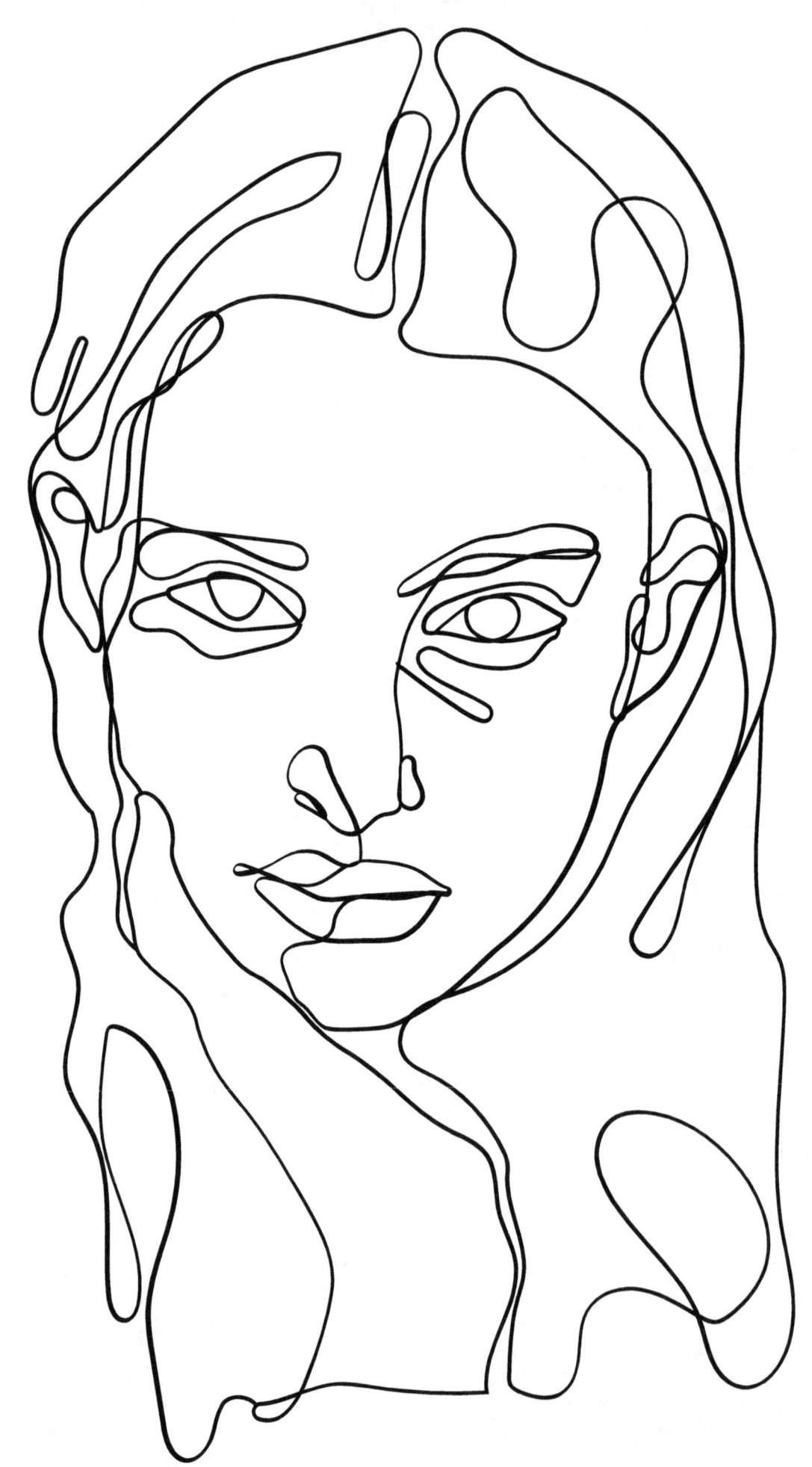

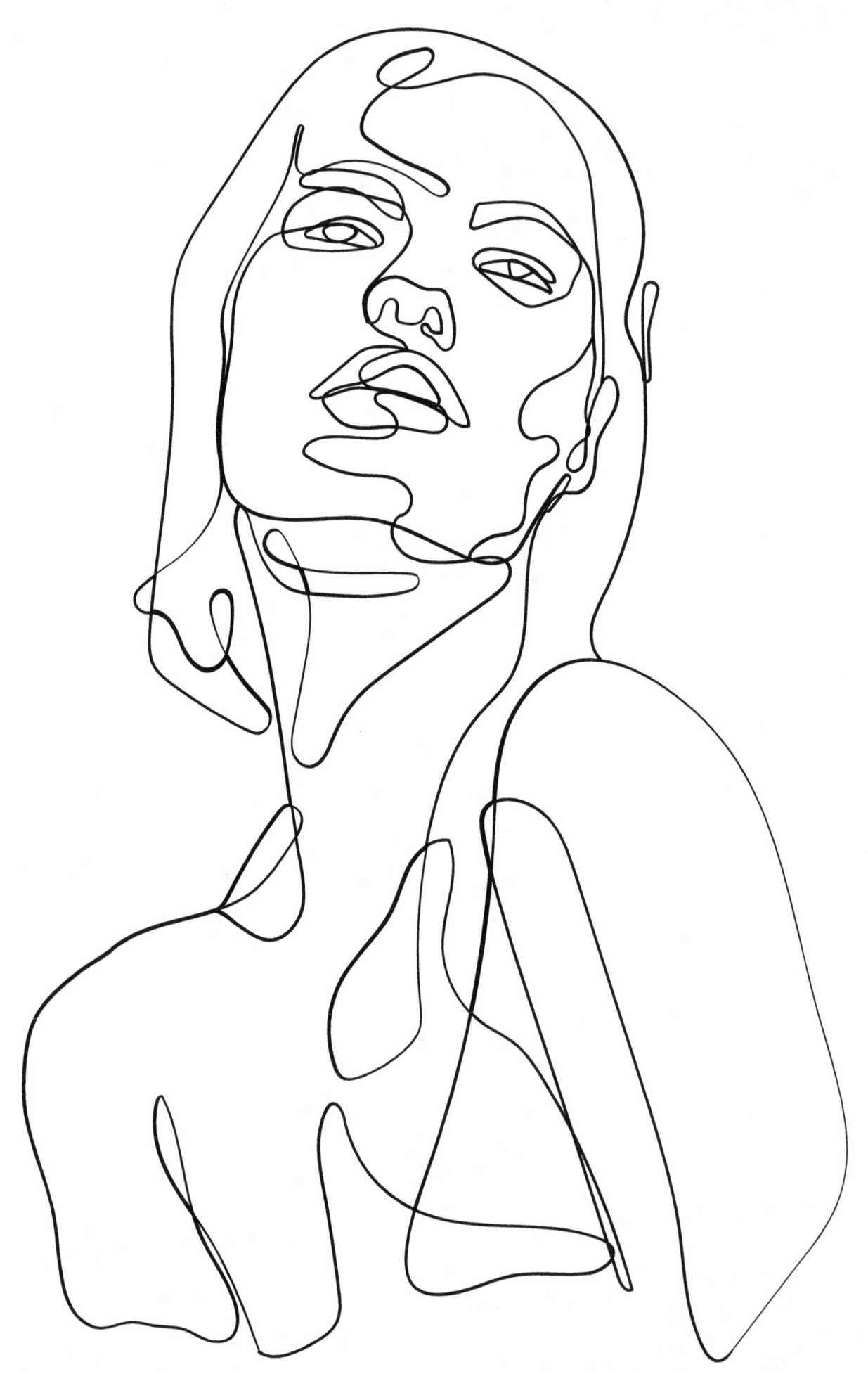

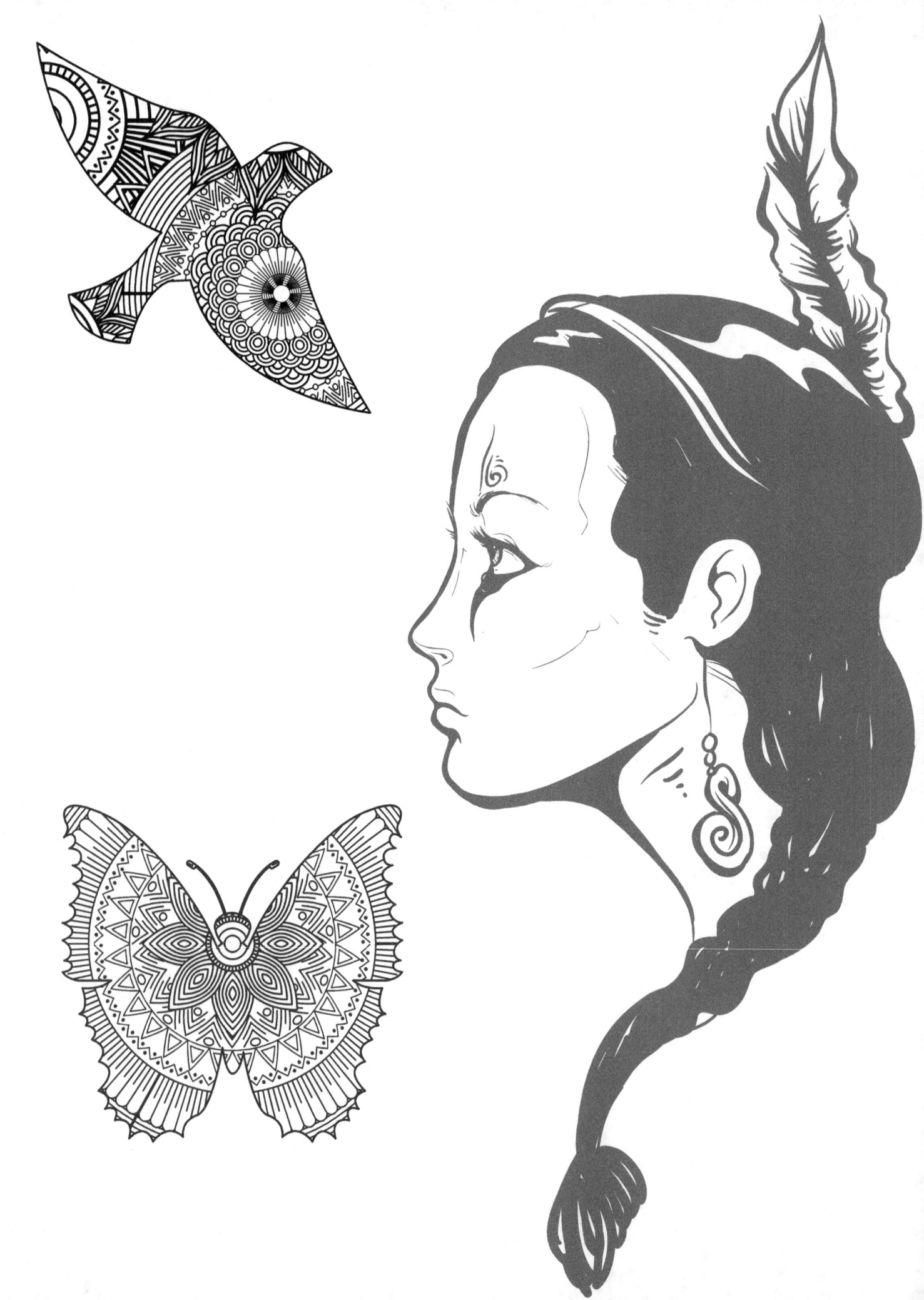

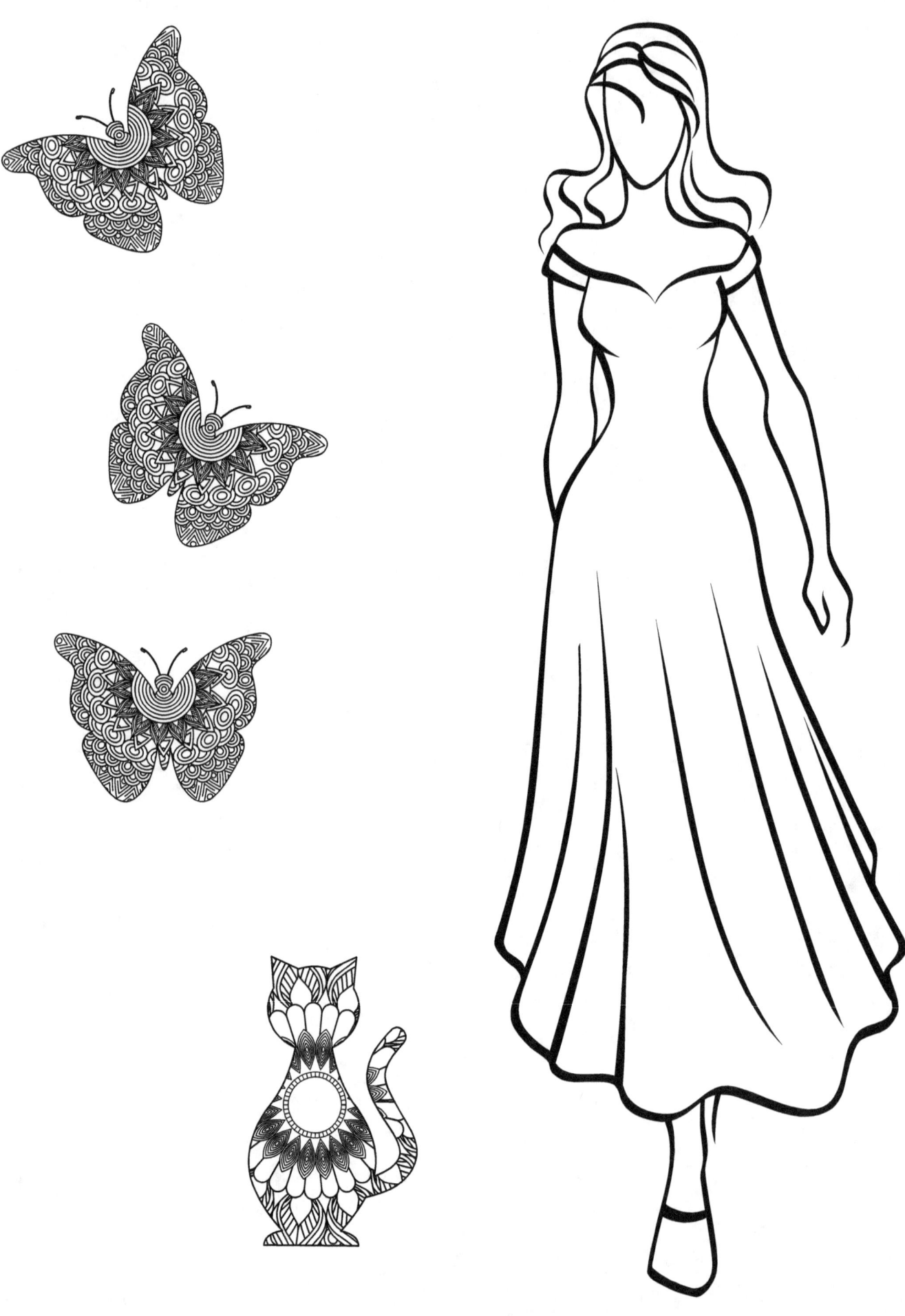

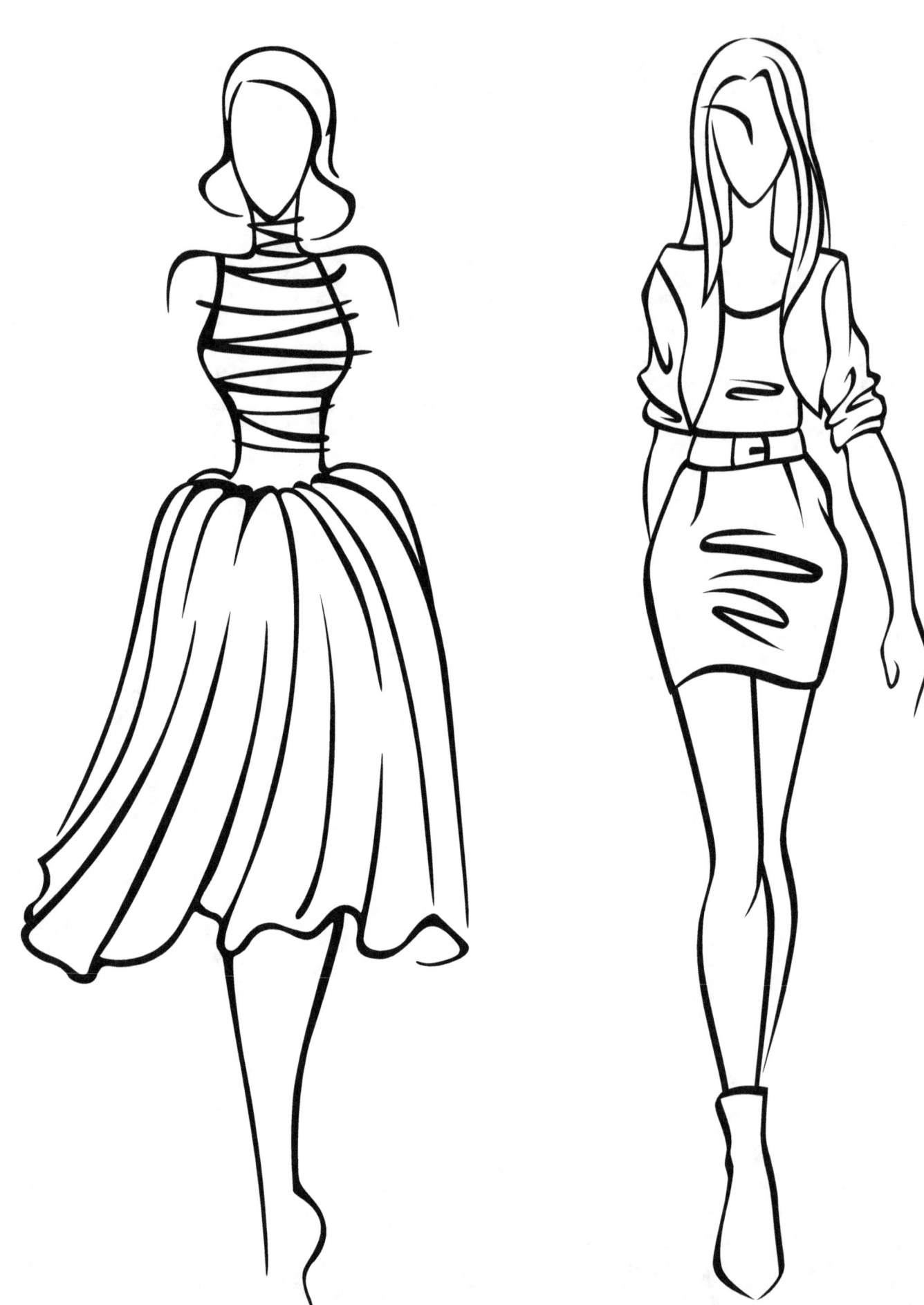

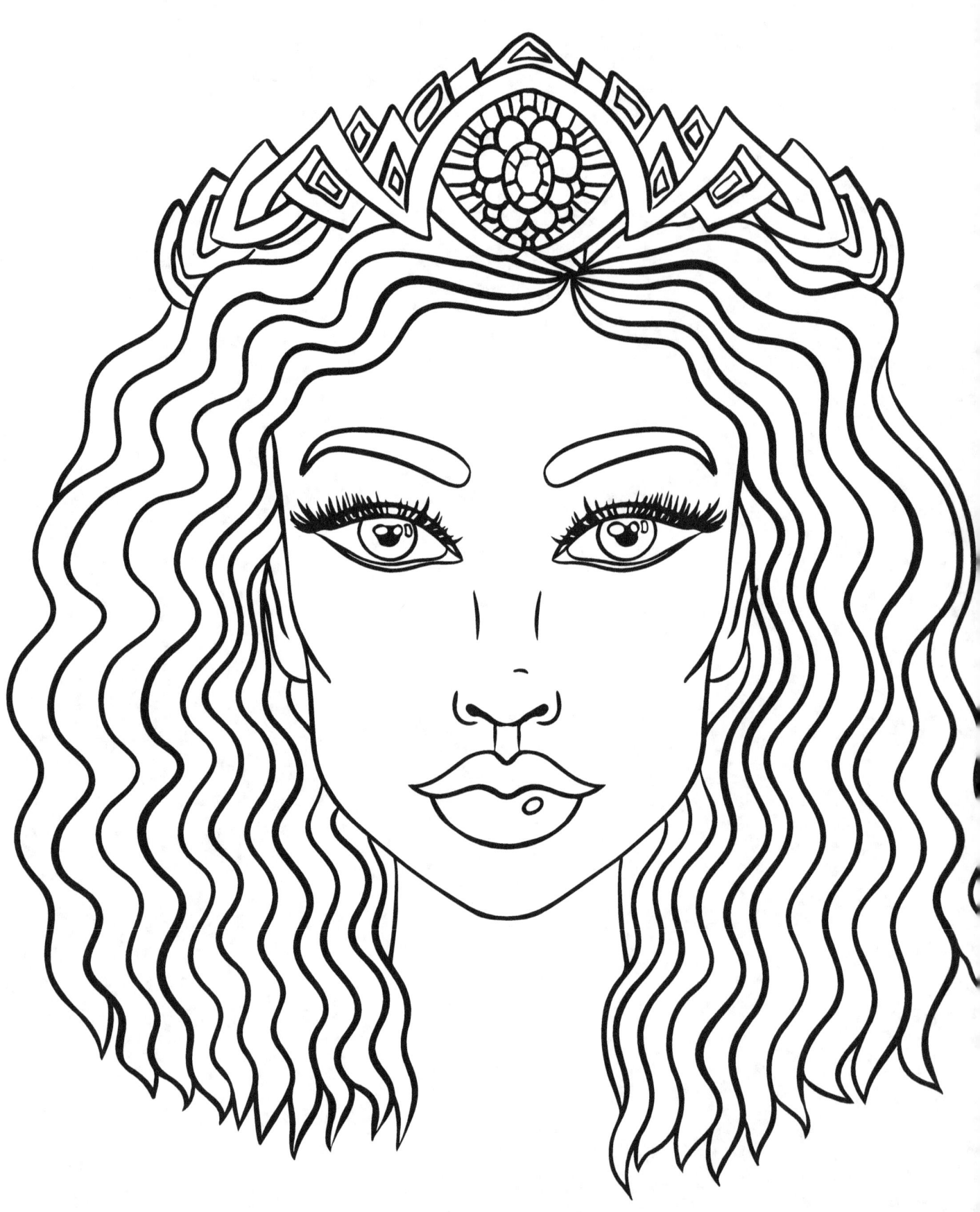

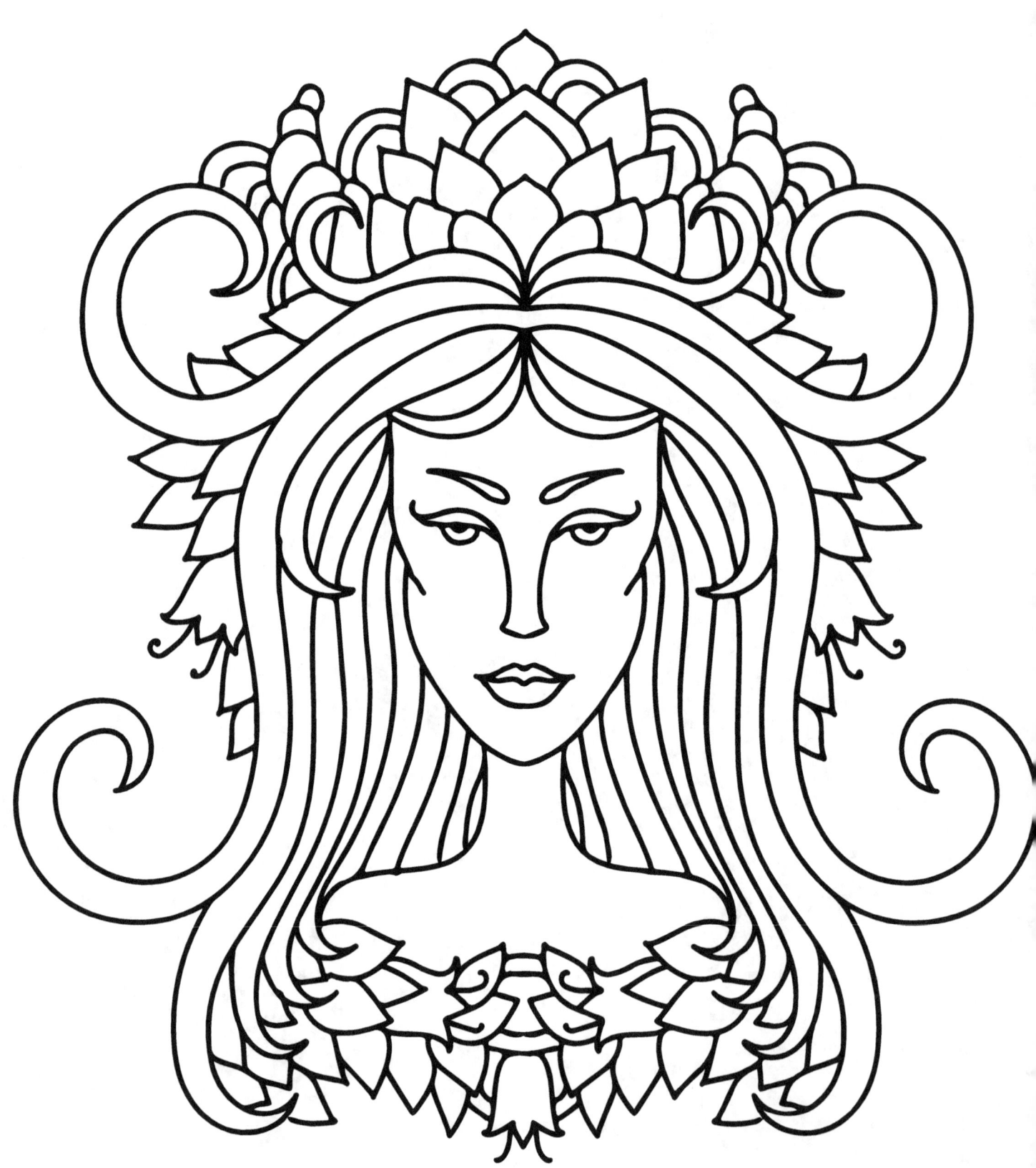

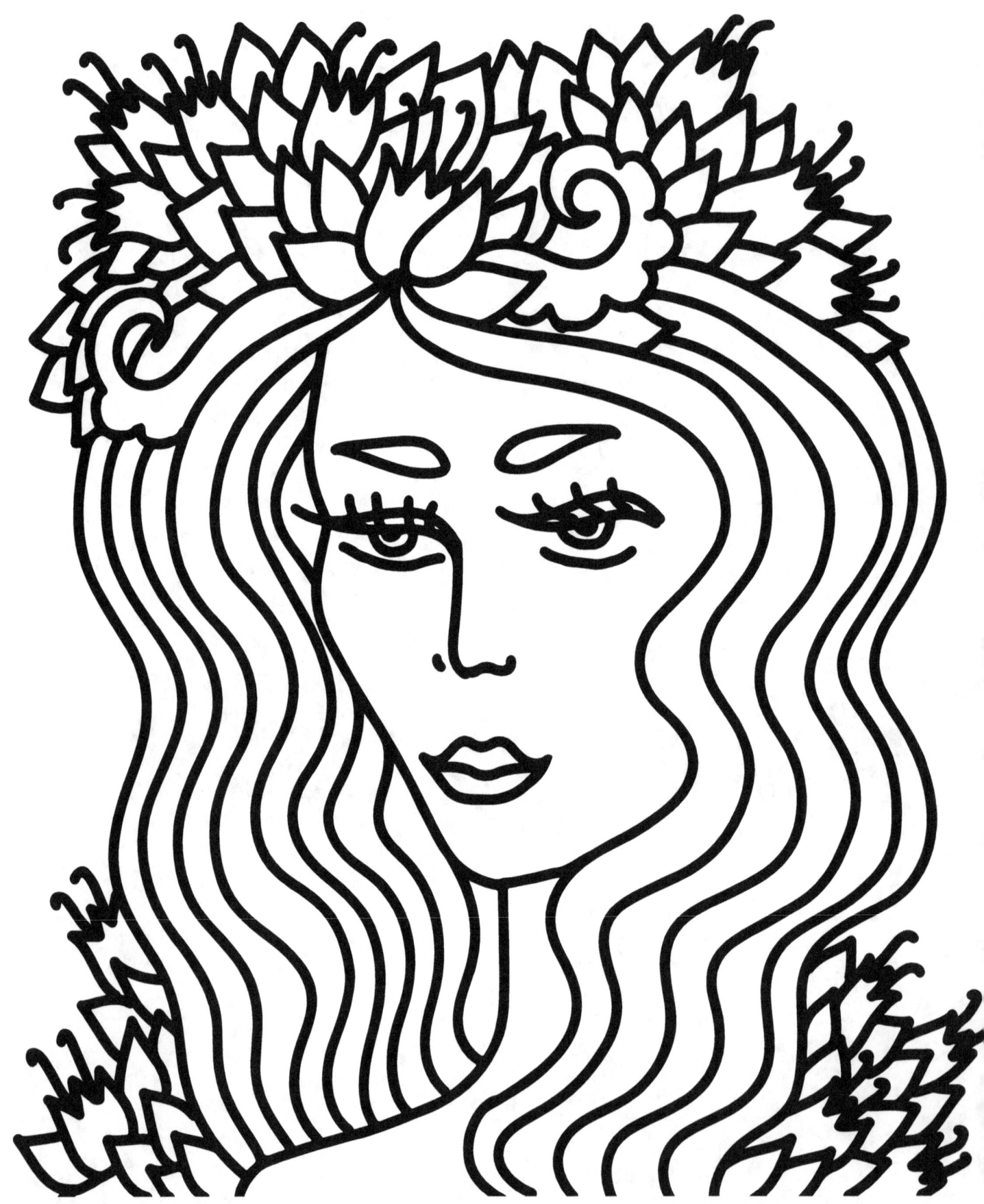

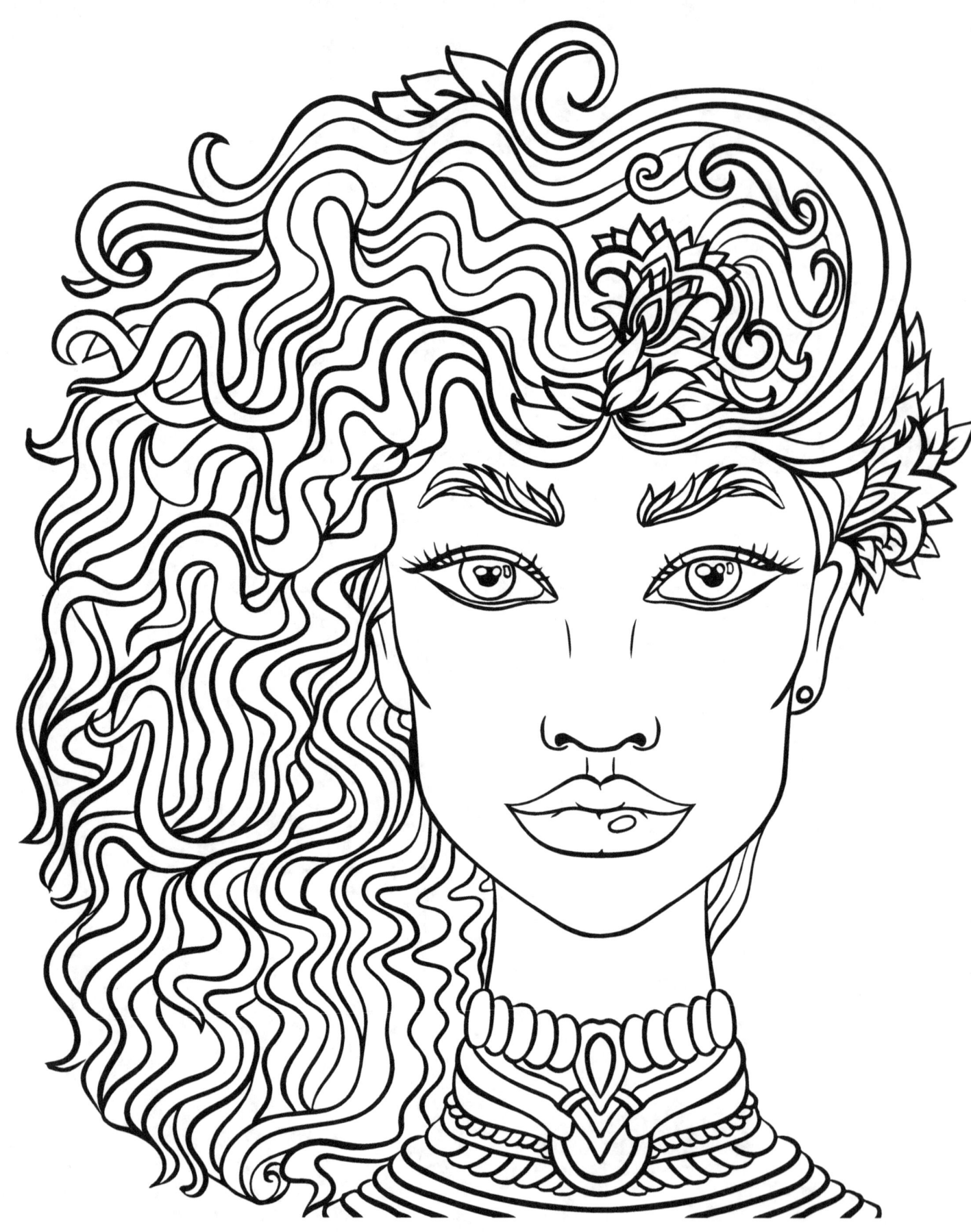

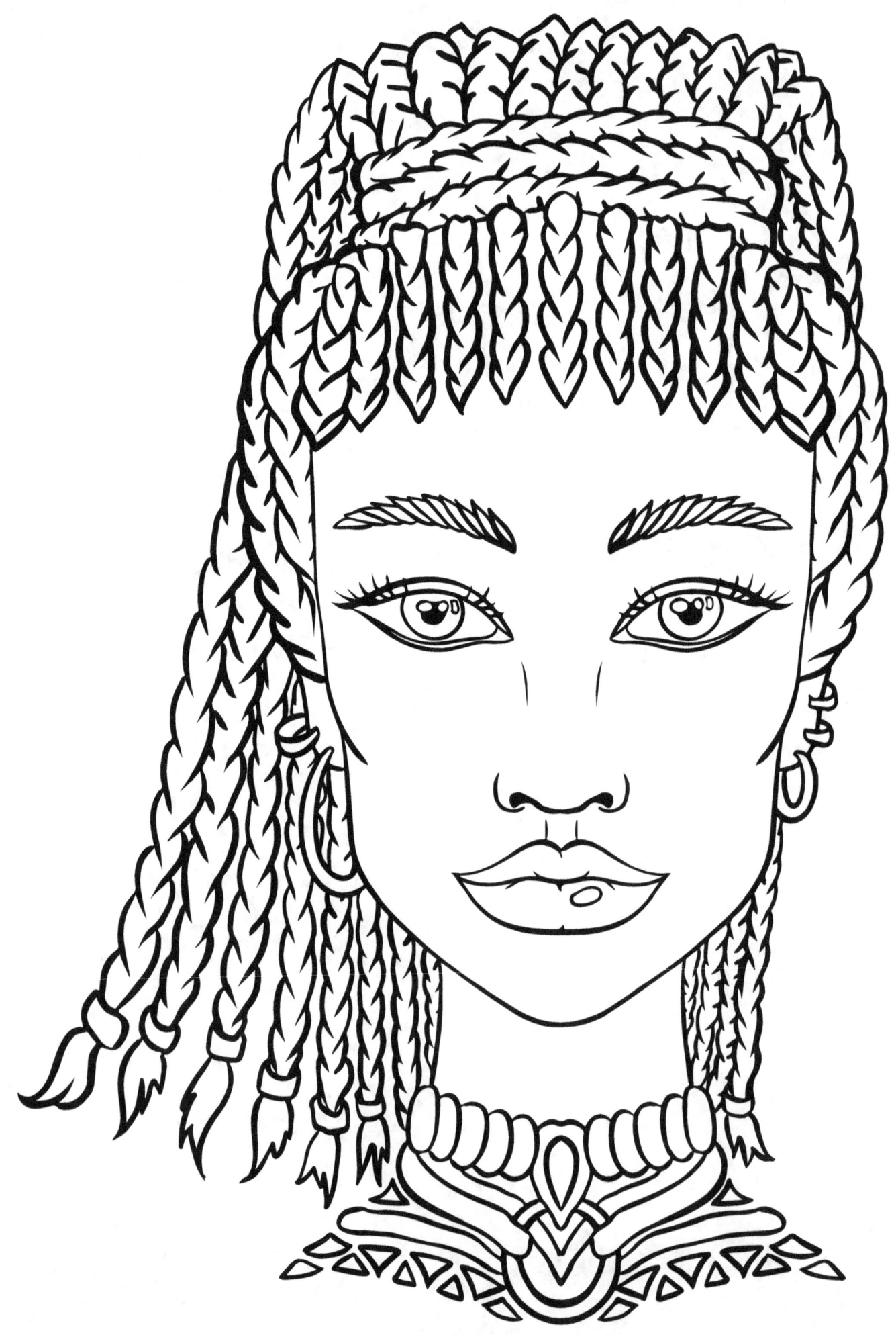

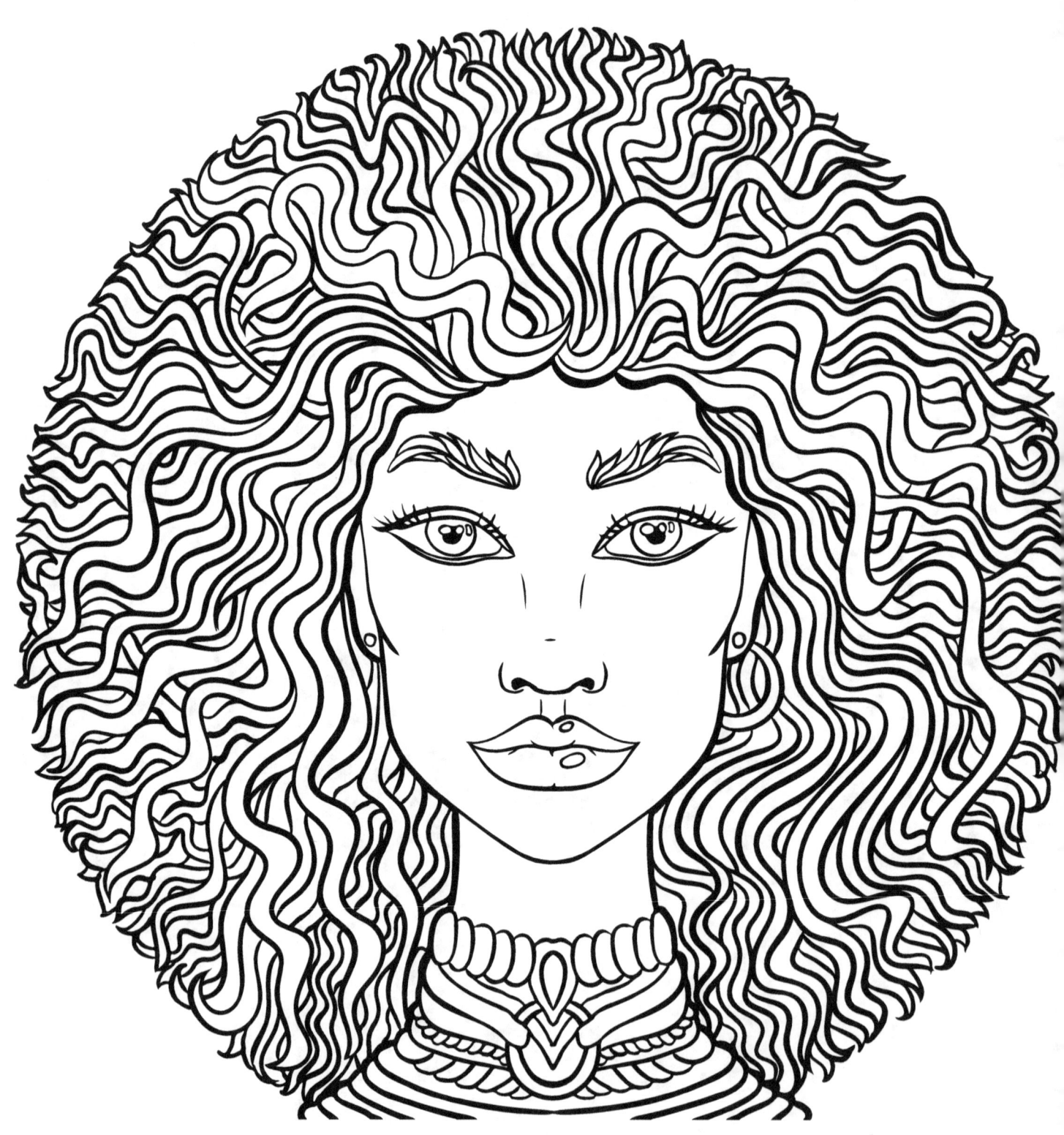

thank you

. . . .

www.ingramcontent.com/pod-product-compliance
Lightning Source LLC
Chambersburg PA
CBHW081704220526
45466CB00009B/2875